NEW VANGUARD 313

FOREIGN PANTHERS

The Panzer V in British, Soviet, French and other service 1943–58

MERLIN ROBINSON & THOMAS SEIGNON

ILLUSTRATED BY
HENRY MORSHEAD

OSPREY PUBLISHING

Bloomsbury Publishing Plc

Kemp House, Chawley Park, Cumnor Hill, Oxford OX2 9PH, UK

29 Earlsfort Terrace, Dublin 2, Ireland

1385 Broadway, 5th Floor, New York, NY 10018, USA

E-mail: info@ospreypublishing.com

www.ospreypublishing.com

OSPREY is a trademark of Osprey Publishing Ltd

First published in Great Britain in 2022

A catalogue record for this book is available from the British Library.

ISBN: PB 9781472831811; eBook: 9781472832009

ePDF 9781472831996; XML: 9781472831989

22 23 24 25 26 10 9 8 7 6 5 4 3 2 1

Index by Angela Hall
Typeset by PDQ Digital Media Solutions, Bungay, UK
Printed and bound in India by Replika Press Private Ltd.

Osprey Publishing supports the Woodland Trust, the UK's leading woodland conservation charity.

To find out more about our authors and books visit **www.ospreypublishing.com**. Here you will find extracts, author interviews, details of forthcoming events and the option to sign up for our newsletter.

Acknowledgements

Our thanks to Simon Dunstan, Nicolas Couderc, Steven Zaloga, Peter Brown, Jeff Plowman, the staff of the SHD de Chatellerault, Nicholas Moran, Ed Harris, Péter Mujzer, Stefan Karlsson, Fraser Gray, Bohumír Kudlička, Josef Žikeš, Tim Strickland and the staff of the Musée des Blindés de Saumur for their kind help in the preparation of this book. Much of the Panther's enduring mystique originated in its generally excellent performance in battle on the Eastern Front, in Italy and in North-West Europe during the last two years of World War II. The separate evaluations of this significant tank design by its enemies revealed its strengths and flaws. This study has benefitted from the hard work of many historians in multiple languages who have collected and collated details from archival data. Some of this information lay for years ignored, while some was hitherto unavailable – and in the absence of documentary evidence, mystique can sometimes generate myths. We thank these individual historians for making available each fragment of a larger story. Even today, the post-war story of the Panther is still not 100 per cent definitive. Unseen evidence may yet exist over six decades since the final disappearance of Panthers from the world's armies in the late 1950s. These researchers are named in the source list and bibliography, but to all of them (and to any we have omitted), the authors of this book express their gratitude.

CONTENTS

FOREIGN PANTHERS

The Panzer V in British, Soviet, French and other service 1943–58

INTRODUCTION

Of Germany's wartime armoured vehicles, amongst the best regarded by its opponents was the Sd.Kfz. 171 Panzerkampfwagen V Panther. So powerful was the Panther's Rheinmetall-Borsig 7.5cm KwK 42 high-velocity gun and so thick its frontal armour that captured Panthers were sought for evaluation by all the Allied armies. Panthers in running condition were even employed where possible against the Wehrmacht. This practice was adopted on both the Eastern and Western fronts, and technical interest in the Panther persisted after the war, so evaluation of the type continued. Elements of the Panther's design inspired several armies in the development of post-war medium tanks on the way forward to the main battle tank concept in the 1950s. Such is the lasting renown surrounding Germany's late-war tank designs that a full record of the Panther's use by its allies and erstwhile enemies is long overdue. The accepted history of the Panther as a post-war weapon was long coloured by the estimations of Western intelligence services (or by misinformation), which aggrandized its limited military significance.

PANTHERS IN THE SERVICE OF AXIS ALLIES

Fascist Italy was the first foreign country to express an interest in adopting the Panther, which was no surprise considering the general obsolescence of Italian wartime medium tank designs. In February 1943, in the hope of helping Italian industry to field a competitive battle tank for the country's army, FIAT-Ansaldo was given permission to produce a local version of the Panther by the Panther's principal designer, MAN. This agreement included a technical advisory body of engineers from MAN to help set up production in Italy. The project was still only at the stage of planning and discussions when the Italian surrender came in September 1943. Romania

A Panther being demonstrated to officers of the Honved in 1944. The Panther was coveted by the Romanians, Italians, Hungarians and even by the Japanese for its balance of firepower, protection and speed. (Péter Mujzer)

German instructors demonstrating the Panther to Hungarian armoured corps officers during the summer of 1944 at Esztergomtábor. The Hungarians received their first five Panthers from the Germans in late August 1944. Between ten and 12 more Panthers were received over the following months, being used by the two Hungarian armoured divisions against Soviet and Romanian forces in Galicia, Transylvania and in the defence of the Hungarian capital. The Hungarians made very effective use of these German tanks, alongside the Panzer IV and a small number of Tiger Ausf Es. (Péter Mujzer)

also approached the Reich in the hope of purchasing Panthers, and while transactions may have been completed, Romania's defection to the Allied side came before any were delivered.

Japan too had been privy to the early development of the Panther Ausf D (and of the Tiger Ausf E), and requested a production licence in April 1943. The following month, Japan requested to purchase a reference sample of each vehicle to study series production. Because the military situation and the logistics of shipping 45- and 56-ton vehicles from Germany to Japan were by then impossible, it is believed that any monies paid were quickly reimbursed.

The *Honved* (Hungarian Army) was the only ally of the Third Reich to use the Panther in combat. Officers of the Honved's HTI (*Haditechnikai Intézet*, or military technology institute) had first been shown Panther prototypes at Kummesdorf in early 1943. Bitter experience had proven that their own Turan medium tank was obsolete, and the Hungarians sought to purchase sufficient Tigers and Panthers to bolster their 1st and 2nd Armoured Divisions. Second-hand Tigers and new Panthers were provided in only small numbers to Hungary, Germany having to prioritize the available vehicles for its own hard-pressed army. The Panther was demonstrated to Honved armoured corps troops on several occasions during the early part of 1944. Sources suggest that during July 1944, five Panther Ausf Gs were sold and delivered to Hungary, and these were sent on (along with a shipment of Panzer IVs) to bolster the 2nd Hungarian Armoured Division then fighting in Galicia.

The Panthers were assigned to the 1st Company, 3/1 Tank Battalion of the Hungarian 2nd Armoured Division. They were in action the next day at Ludus against the 21st Romanian Division. On 15 September 1944, the Panthers led a counter-attack mounted by the 3/1 Tank Battalion at Torda. The following day, the 1st Company was able to save the 3/1 Battalion by disrupting a Soviet tank attack. On 22 September, the Panthers managed to destroy the better part of an enemy tank battalion, although the first of the precious Panthers was also destroyed in combat. On 24 September, two Panthers (by then the last of the original five in operational condition) were mustered with a small force of Turans and Panzer IVs left from the 3rd Tank Regiment. These were used in a final counter-attack against the Soviets in the Peterlakat Valley on 26 September, prior to the division's withdrawal from the valley.

The Panthers represented only a small proportion of tanks deployed in the Hungarian 2nd Armoured Division, but these were boldly used before the division withdrew from Transylvania on 8 October. They had managed to destroy 11 enemy tanks and 17 anti-tank guns in the Torda area between 15 September and 5 October 1944 for the loss of three of the Panthers. A further delivery of Panthers to the Honved came later that year (numbering ten or possibly 12 vehicles from the former Romanian order). In early December 1944, the 2nd Armoured Division could still count four Panthers on its strength. Hungarian crews sent for training on Panthers (and other German types) in Germany in January 1945 for the reinforcement of the Honved's armoured divisions were eventually sent back to Hungary without their promised German tanks as the war situation deteriorated. Photographic evidence suggests that some of the Honved's Panthers may have survived to participate in the defence of Budapest.[1]

ASSESSING THE THREAT: ALLIED EVALUATIONS 1943–44

Captured Panthers were subjected to exhaustive technical evaluation by their captors, driven as much to determine their strength as to discover their weaknesses. The Panther was not unique in this regard, as every other German tank type – from the little Panzer I to the heavy Tigers – was subjected to the same regime of tests and evaluations by the British, American and Russian armies.

Soviet evaluation

The first Panthers captured by the Red Army were the early-production Ausf D type blooded during the Kursk offensive in July 1943. These Panthers were deployed in haste (without adequate trials) to provide a technically superior medium tank to the Soviet T-34. Most of the Panthers captured by the Red Army during Operation *Citadel* were lost due to mechanical failure, engine fires or mine damage. In their first actions, at least five Panthers were lost due to engine fires from ruptured fuel pumps. Soviet evaluation of the type began on 20 July 1943, and the preliminary results of their assessments (consisting of photographs, specifications and some observations regarding combat use) were shared with the Western Allies in September and October 1943. An exhaustive internal Soviet report was also produced, based on close examination of an early-production Panther Ausf D (*fahrgestell*, or chassis number, 210055).

This vehicle was not captured in running order, but the report praised the Panther's design in terms of its powerful armament, its high-quality optics and the layout of its sloped armour. Subsequent Soviet evaluations at Kubinka of captured Panther Ausf Ds number 824 and 732 (the latter being turret tactical numbers rather than chassis numbers) recovered from the Kursk battlefield and returned to running condition indicated that the suspension

1   See Mujzer, Péter, *Operational History of The Hungarian Armoured Troops in World War II*, Kagero, Lublin (2018), pp.94–100, 104, 121.

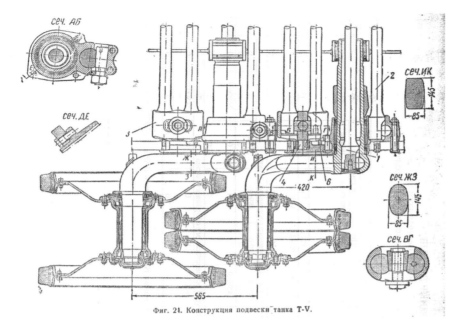

сеч. АБ

сеч. ИК

сеч. ДЕ

сеч. ЖЗ

-420

-565

сеч. ВГ

Фиг. 24. Конструкция подвески танка T-V.

Diagram from the T-V *Pantera* manual prepared in late 1943 by the Red Army in the hope that the Panther might be captured in sufficient numbers to justify equipping units with these powerful vehicles. The reality was that only a few Panthers were ever in use with the Red Army during the war, due to logistic and mechanical factors. The T-V designation was altered to T-5 by the Bulgarian and Romanian armies when they eventually received captured Panthers from the USSR, which were used until the 1950s. CIA documents suggest that Western intelligence mistook the Panther for a far more important weapon in the Eastern European armies of the late 1940s and early 1950s than was the actual case. (Collection Thomas Seignon)

and wide track gave excellent cross-country mobility. The gun and optics were of high quality and the Red Army found the 45-ton Panther was a fine gunnery platform. Soviet conclusions were not all positive, however, regarding the powerplant and transmission as being overtaxed with little scope for further development. Firing trials followed with 45mm, 76.2mm, 6-pdr and 85mm D5 guns. None of these weapons could reliably penetrate the front of the Panther, but 122mm D25T, 152mm ML20 and 100mm D10 guns all defeated the Panther's glacis and turret front at ranges exceeding 1,000m. Further evaluation of the later Ausf A and Ausf G models continued as opportunities presented in 1944, and more firing trials were conducted in order to determine the means of neutralizing the new tank in combat. The development of the IS-2, T-43, SU-100, T-34-85 and T-44 tanks and tank destroyers all included firing tests against captured Panthers.

At least 29 Panther Ausf Ds were captured during the course of Operation *Citadel*, but very few of these were suitable for returning to service due to mechanical component failure and general unreliability. Their use posed important logistical problems in an army whose tanks were mostly diesel-fuelled by mid-1943, which made them a problematic and unpopular 'trophy' with the higher Soviet commanders. Designated 'T-V' (or T-5 in Arabic numerals), the Red Army anticipated capture of sufficient '*Pantera*' (written Пантера in Cyrillic) to merit the preparation of an official Russian-language manual for the type published during 1944. The quickly accepted reality was that captured Panthers could only be used for short periods where fuel, ammunition and the Panther's mechanical health permitted.

British evaluation

In Italy, a knocked-out Panther was examined locally by representatives of all of the major Western Allies in March 1944. Analysis proved that the Panther was significantly superior in armour and firepower to the Sherman and Churchill tanks. Nonetheless, its rarity and its adoption so soon after

Panther 433 (*Fahrgestel* chassis number 213101) was supplied to the British Government by the USSR for evaluation following its capture in the Kursk area in July 1943. Arriving in May 1944, '433' was tested as extensively as possible over a two-week period, but due to the fact that this tank was a very early production Ausf D repaired by the Soviets prior to shipment (with only other destroyed Panthers as a source for parts), its mechanical state was poor. At around the time that '433' arrived in England, the British Eighth Army encountered the Panther and the Pantherturm fortifications in the Hitler Line in Italy. (Crown Copyright)

Several of the features of '433' particular to the early Ausf D Panthers seen here as presented in FVPE Report No. FT1391, were improved later during production. Panther '433' is shown shortly after arrival in the United Kingdom with its gun clamped for shipment. From this angle we can see the original-pattern commander's cupola, the pistol and shell loading ports in the turret side and some of the weld details invisible on later tanks delivered with zimmerit non-magnetic anti-mine coating. (Crown Copyright)

the Tiger Ausf E caused some misconceptions in Allied intelligence. Up until June 1944, American intelligence mistook the Panther as an alternate heavy tank type to the Tiger rather than as a medium tank to replace the Panzer IV.

The Soviets were uncharacteristically generous in providing the British Army with one Panther recovered from the Kursk battlefield, but its repair and subsequent transit to Britain took over seven months. Panthers were by then being encountered in limited numbers in Italy by the British Eighth Army. Damaged Panthers were recovered and evaluated locally by Free French, British and American forces in Italy during the same period. Panther turrets emplaced separately as field fortifications (*Pantherturm*) were widely encountered during the assault on the Hitler Line in May 1944. The KwK 42 7.5cm gun proved capable of destroying with ease M4 Sherman medium tanks as well as the more heavily armoured Churchill infantry tanks.

A Panther Ausf D (chassis number 213101, still bearing a prominent German tactical marking '433' on its turret) arrived in England in May 1944. The Soviets had repaired it to driveable condition prior to shipment, using parts cannibalized from other vehicles prior to shipment. This vehicle (known hereafter as '433') was probably not a pristine mechanical specimen. The '433' was evaluated by the Fighting Vehicles Proving Establishment (FVPE) in mobility trials around the unit's base at Bovington in Dorset alongside a Churchill Mk VII, a Sherman and a Cromwell. The gun and mantlet were then removed for separate evaluation and suspension trials continued with steel weights attached to compensate. The Panther developed hydraulic system problems and a minor engine fire during these tests. British reports concerning '433' and its ergonomics, mobility and suspension were largely critical in nature. Transmission problems affecting the third gear ended the

Because '433' was the only Panther in British hands at the time of its receipt, its 7.5cm KwK 42 gun and mantlet were dismounted and replaced by a weighted structure. Mobility trials with '433' drew criticism from the Fighting Vehicle Proving Establishment personnel evaluating it. The British report that followed these trials compared this Panther's battlefield mobility negatively to the Churchill Mk VII, while its suspension was singled out as unsatisfactory: '[T]he opinion of all members of F.V.P.E. staff who have ridden across country on the tank is that the suspension is not good.' (Crown Copyright)

trials prematurely, requiring workshop repair. Since the Panther was noted for its excellent floatation and smooth ride in Soviet reports, this suggests that some of the repairs undertaken to make '433' driveable were not enough to render it back to operational standard.

On 28 June, a mileage test was undertaken but was cut short due to mechanical problems which required further maintenance. Issues developed with the fuel system, and after the engine was switched off, '433' suffered a backfire, followed by an explosion and catastrophic engine fire. The '433' had endured only 15 days of evaluation by that time, much of which had been spent in maintenance. The unarmed hulk with armour plate welded to the turret front underwent firing trials to determine the best means of defeating the Panther's well-sloped glacis armour. The difficulties presented by the Panther's angled frontal armour had by then manifested themselves on both the Italian and Normandy battlefields.

British weapons testing against a captured Panther Ausf G, an Ausf G turret and other captured Panthers continued in October and November 1944 at Shoeburyness, Essex. In these trials, the Panthers were subjected to 75mm, 17-pdr, 6-pdr, 20mm and PIAT fire (amongst other weapons). From the front, the Panther was only vulnerable to the 17-pdr below 1,500m with armour-piercing discarding sabot (APDS) or below 800m with armour-piercing capped ballistic cap (APCBC) ammunition. Other weapons could destroy the Panther from the sides and rear, or by deflecting hits on the mantlet into the roof of the driver's compartment. Inconsistent hardness and quality control of armour plate used to construct Panthers was one conclusion derived from these tests. The Panther's armour hardness tended towards brittleness in some cases, and was reported to be of poorer quality than contemporary British armour plate.

Once '433' had suffered a catastrophic engine fire during fairly brief trials in late July 1944, it was used as a hard target to analyze the effects of Allied anti-tank weapons on what had by then proven to be a very difficult opponent in combat. In order to get the maximum life out of the target, plates were welded over the turret front to simulate a mantlet, and over the glacis. (Crown Copyright)

American evaluation of a captured Panther Ausf A at Aberdeen Proving Ground in Maryland. The US Army extensively evaluated an unknown number of Panthers in the USA during 1944 and 1945 (likely over a dozen) and even after the war ended. Four of these survive in collections today. (NARA, with thanks to Steven Zaloga)

American evaluation

The US Army did not expect the Germans to use such an expensive tank as the Panther as the main equipment for entire panzer divisions prior to D-Day. In Normandy, however, they discovered that the Panther was intended to replace the Panzer IV as Germany's standard medium tank, which increased the urgency for finding a means of defeating the Panther. American 3in., 90mm M1 and 76mm M1A1 guns had been tested alongside the British and American 75mm and the British QF 17-pdr in firing trials against plate targets (simulating the frontal armour protection expected on German tanks, including the Panther) at Shoeburyness on 23 May 1944. The plates used in the trial differed in hardness from the standards used in German plate, and in general engendered a false sense of security regarding the capabilities of the new American 76mm M1 and 3in. guns against the Panther. In Normandy, the American tankers found Panthers in greater profusion than expected, and these proved difficult to destroy in combat.

Early evaluation of captured Panthers by the US Army in France was focused on testing the various American tank guns to see which could and could not penetrate the German tank using the whole range of available ammunition. Firing trials were also conducted at Aberdeen Proving Ground. (NARA)

The US Army captured several Panthers in the opening month of the Normandy campaign, and the first Panther employed in a firing test to

determine its vulnerability to standard US weapons (and to the British 17-pdr) was evaluated in-theatre on 10 July 1944 at Balleroy. The Panther's frontal armour proved extremely difficult to penetrate, which caused the matter to be escalated. Firing tests with the whole panoply of American anti-tank weapons were then conducted by the US First Army between 12 July and 30 July at Isigny. Results were disappointing, with the exception of the M1A1 90mm gun firing AP M77 rounds. The trial results suggested that the American 76mm and 3in. guns were only capable of penetrating the Panther's turret frontally at dangerously close ranges. The need for a counter to the threat posed by the Panther's sloped armour was escalated to army group level.

Firing trials were held again by the 12th Army Group on 20 and 21 August, again at Isigny. The trials evaluated the performance of the American 76mm – using APC and HVAP-T (high-velocity armour-piercing tracer) ammunition – versus the British 17-pdr gun (firing APCBC and APDS) against the frontal armour of three Panthers. The 76mm gun failed to penetrate consistently, even at ranges below 200m, and the majority of the shots were deflected. British APDS ammunition proved much less accurate than any of the types tested for the American gun, but achieved better penetration when it actually hit. The test also proved that 76mm HVAP could penetrate the Panther's turret frontally from ranges under 500m, which resulted in an emergency shipment of 1,000 76mm T4 HVAP rounds being made from the United States to the army in Normandy. The arrival of more 76mm HVAP ammunition and the M36 tank destroyer, with its 90mm gun, in September 1944 proved to be the ultimate American answer to fighting the Panther on anything like even terms.

American evaluation of the Panther at the unit level continued into the winter of 1944 as opportunities permitted. These focused on finding its weaknesses and the best methods to capitalize on these to pass on as 'lessons learned' to combat units. Several reports survive from combat units describing how Panthers were defeated in action, as well as the results of local trials conducted against captured Panthers some time after those carried out at Isigny. One report written by the commanding officer of the 628th Tank Destroyer Battalion to the 5th Armoured Division's artillery commander, dated 8 December 1944, described an action where an M36 tank destroyer successfully knocked out a Panther with eight 90mm hits:

> The 90mm gun will penetrate a Mark V at a range of 1200 yards if the shell strikes at a favourable angle. A single round fired from the 90mm gun will not penetrate the frontal plate of … a Mark V if the slightest deflection angle is present. However, a solid hit on the turret can jam the turret.[2]

American infantry anti-tank weapons were also tested out at around the same time in North-West Europe. The 57mm M1 gun (essentially an American-built 6-pdr anti-tank gun) proved capable of penetrating the Panther's side armour at 300 yards' range in tests conducted in the Schalbach area by the 776th Tank Destroyer Battalion, using a gun belonging to the 71st Infantry Regiment. The gun was also capable of severely damaging the Panther's suspension and tracks. The conclusions noted that the 57mm anti-tank gun was most effective if used from ranges below 500 yards and advised that

The Panther target seen here has each penetration carefully numbered and is being looked over by American soldiers. American trial results quickly identified a wide range of plate hardness levels and the presence of brittle armour plate in many of the captured Panthers. (NARA)

2   See Gallagher, Lieutenant-Colonel W.J., 'Effect of 90mm Gun on Enemy Tanks. Headquarters 628th Tank Destroyer Battalion', (SP), United States Army, 8 December 1944.

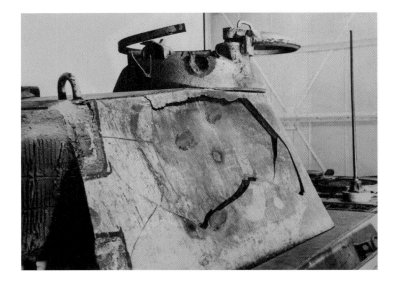

firing from longer ranges would only betray the gun's positions. Shots against the front of the Panther's armour were deflected or otherwise failed to penetrate. The unenviable experience of a gun crew waiting for a Panther to advance so close and to expose its weaker side armour under actual combat conditions was not commented upon further in the report.[3]

Another report described use of the 57mm bazooka's anti-tank rockets on a Panther knocked out by the 776th Tank Destroyer Battalion. The trial was intended to determine the best means of engaging the Panther with the standard infantry anti-tank weapon of the time. The report noted that the turret sides and rear could be penetrated by well-placed rockets, but that attempts to immobilize the Panther were more difficult due to the layered roadwheels and stout tracks (both of which could be damaged, but not to the extent where the vehicle could be definitively put out of action). The rear of the Panther's hull could be penetrated by the bazooka's rockets, but the prominent exhaust mountings, stowage boxes and fittings could all prematurely detonate the rockets. Frontal engagements were not advised because of the steeply angled glacis:

> Upon the front armour, it is difficult to get an effective burst, as the slope of the armour will ricochet the rocket. No perpendicular hits were obtained during the trial.[4]

In January 1945, the US Ordnance Department published a handbook on the 90mm M3 gun ammunition types following official trials of the effectiveness of 90mm HVAP T30E16 and 90mm armour-piercing shot T33 rounds against an Ausf A (conducted at Aberdeen Proving Ground in Maryland). The photos in the handbook showed a Panther glacis effectively stoven in by multiple direct hits around the hull machine-gun mounting, which cracked the glacis plate to the point of failure.

The US Army held a large stock of captured German armoured vehicles by the war's end, gathered into massive yards in France, Belgium and Germany. A number of captured Panthers in operational condition (and as incomplete specimens) were transported to Aberdeen Proving Ground and evaluated after the war in Europe ended. Unique amongst these were the incomplete mild steel prototype hull of the Panther 2 proposed in 1943 as a more heavily armoured follow-on to the Panther Ausf D. This vehicle included a suspension system which employed Tiger Ausf B components, including

This photo clearly shows the same problem on the plates making up the turret side on a captured Panther Ausf A or G. The issue of brittle plate came as a result of variation in production methods and due to substitutions in the metallurgical processes as reserves of strategic materials were used up in 1944 and 1945. The firing trials conducted by the US Army at Isigny were important in forcing Army Ordnance's hand in the reprioritization of ammunition development to enable the 76mm-gunned M4A1 and M4A3 to take on the Panther. The underestimation of the Panther as a threat came not only because it was such a large (and presumably expensive) tank – which convinced some that the Panther would only be encountered in small numbers – but also because the 23 May 1944 firing tests at Shoeburyness ignored some of the characteristics of German armour metallurgy. (NARA)

3   See Wadle, Major L. J., 'Report of Effectiveness of 57mm Antitank Gun Against Enemy Armour', United States Army, 12 December 1944. See Stiver, Major E. N., 'Memorandum to 5th Tank Destroyer Group: Bazooka Test on Mk.V', United States Army.
4   See Stiver, Major E. N., 'Memorandum to 5th Tank Destroyer Group: Bazooka Test on Mk.V', United States Army, 15 December 1944.

the road wheels and final drives. It also featured thicker hull side and glacis armour. Because the hull was incomplete at the time of capture and the Panther 2 project had already been abandoned before the end of the war, its evaluation proved to be brief (although the hull was preserved and completed with Ausf G components and an Ausf G turret for the ordnance museum assembled after the war at Aberdeen).

A second experimental Panther variant was also studied by the US Army, designated the Panther Ausf F. One of its most interesting features was the Daimler Benz-designed 'schmalturm', a simplified narrow turret armed with the 7.5cm KwK 44, a Škoda-designed refinement of the 7.5cm Kwk 42 with a shorter recoil and modified breech. The turret was intended for use on Panzer IV and Panther hulls, and was cheaper to build in fewer man hours than the original Panther turret. It was also better armoured, with a 150mm-thick conical mantlet, 120mm-thick turret face and turret sides 60mm thick. The Panther F's hull was a slightly modified Panther Ausf G pattern, armed with an MG42 for the co-driver and with a 40mm-thick hull roof over the driver's and fighting compartments. The commander's cupola was revised to a lower profile and the 7.5cm KwK 44 gun dispensed with the earlier gun's muzzle brake. Production versions were to be fitted with a 1,320mm-wide Zeiss stereoscopic rangefinder, but none of the wartime production *schmalturms* were captured completed to 'service' configuration.

The British 17-pdr (although erratic in terms of accuracy when firing APDS) and the American 90mm gun both proved capable of penetrating the Panther frontally at Isigny. The US Army chose to develop HVAP (high-velocity armour-piercing) ammunition for the 76mm M1 gun as the longer term (and most reliable) solution for their medium tanks, along with the expedited introduction of the M36 tank destroyer. (NARA)

IN COMBAT

The Red Army

Soviet use of captured Panthers as functional combat tanks was always brief. The first recorded use of such a Panther appears in the Belgorod sector on 5 August 1943, at a time when captured ammunition for the KwK 42 must have been in very short supply. In autumn 1943, a captured Panther was employed by the 59th Independent Tank Regiment, but it was noted that the German artillery systematically targeted the captured vehicle, which did not remain operational for long. The excellent KwK 42 7.5cm gun and its gunsight were admired for their firepower and accuracy, allowing engagements at longer ranges than were possible at the time with Soviet tank guns.

Plans to use captured Panthers were also considered at higher levels at this time. In January 1944, the Soviet armoured corps issued directives that suggested captured Panthers could be used where possible, but in reality this was difficult. The Panther's incompatibility with the Red Army's large stock of captured PaK 40 7.5cm ammunition, its dependence on gasoline fuel and above all the shortage of spares for a tank that could be easily damaged by inexperienced drivers proved insurmountable obstacles.

The Red Army employed captured Panthers throughout the last 18 months of fighting on the Eastern Front, but seldom in the kind of numbers once imagined. Panthers were not widely sought by Soviet commanders because of their burdensome maintenance requirements, petrol fuel and because they could not often be repaired once broken down. When used, Soviet tankers took whatever precautions possible to mark their vehicles to avoid friendly fire. The 366th Guards Heavy Artillery SP Regiment operated two captured Panthers during the advance to Lake Balaton in Hungary in 1945. The German crosses and turret numbers were painted over (presumably in 3BO Green), and red stars painted on over large green squares. The outer road wheels were also painted to alter this Panther Ausf G's regular appearance from a distance. (AC)

These same causes were summarized in a report in September 1944, which explained that a captured Panther taken around Zhytomir in January that year by the 3rd Tank Army was being sent for repair at a nearby maintenance battalion before it could be used. Unlike captured Panzer IIIs and Panzer IVs, which were easily rendered operational and were used for relatively long periods where fuel and ammunition were available, the Panther was a special case. Repaired alongside four Panzer IVs, the single Panther was sent into action a few days later with a Red Army crew. It successfully destroyed a Tiger shortly afterwards, but neither the details of this engagement nor the Panther's eventual fate were recorded. Generally, where Panthers were successfully employed for any time by the Soviets, German mechanic prisoners capable of maintaining the type were put to work assisting their captors. A factory in the Kazan area was designated to undertake refurbishment of captured Panthers, but shortage of spares prevented this from happening.

Photographic evidence survives of three *Pantera* being employed by the VIII Guards Tank Corps in August 1944. These were captured by the 59th Guards Tank Brigade and deployed as a company alongside IS-2 tanks in the 62nd Guards Heavy Tank Regiment. In terms of documentary evidence, some of the more interesting surviving reports recount use of individual Panthers by tank units otherwise equipped with Lend-Lease tanks. The 196th Independent Tank Regiment was recorded in its reports in July 1944 to have captured a serviceable Panther which eventually served alongside its Valentines through an advance of 600km. The tank was captured on 6 July 1944 with track damage, and

A **SOVIET T-V *PANTERA***

Probably captured in the drive westwards in the late summer of 1944, this Soviet T-V *Pantera* served with the 366th Guards Heavy Artillery SP Regiment in March 1945. This assault gun regiment operated several captured enemy vehicles, including two Panthers, presumably abandoned in working order by their German crews. Soviet adoption of captured Panthers on the Eastern Front was long presumed, but the Red Army seems never to have implemented the comprehensive rebuilding and reuse scheme considered after the Kursk battles. This Ausf G carried prominent red stars painted over 3BO Green applied on patches of scraped-off zimmerit on the glacis and both turret sides. The outer road wheels were painted solid green to distinguish this tank, but the rest of the vehicle remains in its German three-colour scheme.

This trio of captured Panthers was employed by the Red Army's VIII Guards Tank Corps after their capture from the 5th SS Panzer Division Wiking in 1944. The Soviets captured many Panthers in 1944 and 1945, but used only few of them in actual combat. Most were gathered in holding yards, and were used as targets after the war. Some were eventually transferred to Bulgaria during 1945, and to Romania and Czechoslovakia after the war, where they quietly served into the 1950s. This long life was deceptive: most of their time was spent in storage in deep reserves. (AC)

such were the regiment's losses that the decision was taken locally to keep it in service as long as supplies allowed. It was in action through the following days while the regiment's Valentines took heavy losses, limited additionally by a lack of crewmen familiar with the KwK 42 gun's operation. This Panther eventually broke down irretrievably and was abandoned. The 511th Tank Regiment operated four captured Panthers alongside their Valentines during the same period, although details of their service are scarce.

In some cases, Red Army mechanized units not normally equipped with tanks employed captured panzers, including Panthers. Two Panthers of undetermined type served as part of the equipment of the 51st Independent Motorcycle Regiment, along with five captured Tigers. One Panther Ausf A (apparently numbered 513) was recorded in Red Army service in the battle for the Praga district in Warsaw in August 1944, in a Lieutenant-Colonel Sotnikov's company, during the Soviet advance into the city. In March 1945, during the Lake Balaton offensive in Hungary, the Red Army's 991st Artillery Regiment counted three Panthers alongside its 16 SU-76 self-propelled guns. To reduce the risk of friendly fire, the artillerymen painted the Panthers' turrets in 3BO green and prominently marked them with white-bordered red stars and large tactical markings. Another two captured Panther Ausf Gs were put into service by the 366th Heavy Artillery Regiment (Self-Propelled) in the 47th Army's sector in Hungary in the same period, similarly overpainted. This summary gives a total of less than 20 documented cases where the T-V *Pantera* saw wartime action in Soviet service, and it is likely that other evidence will emerge – but we must accept that fewer captured Panthers served the Red Army than previously supposed.

Resistance Panthers

Remarkably, resistance forces in Poland and France made use of captured Panthers against their former owners during 1944 and 1945, in numbers exceeding those ever used by the British Army or the Free French Forces (*Forces Françaises Libres*, or FFL), which were the only conventional armies on the Western Front to use captured Panthers. Two captured Panthers were used against the Wehrmacht during the Warsaw Uprising. Fighting erupted at 0500hrs on 1 August 1944 when the *Armia Krajowa* (AK, Polish Home Army) began a series of armed attacks on the Warsaw garrison, launching what swiftly became one of the most horrific episodes of World War II.

At that time, the 27th Panzer Regiment of the 19th Panzer Division, equipped with new Panther Ausf As, were in the western part of Warsaw to exchange a number of their Panthers for new G models at the garrison's maintenance facilities. On 2 August, three of the 27th Panzer Regiment's tanks were driving through the city when they were ambushed on Okopowa Street. As the Panthers drove towards the Jewish cemetery, an ambush was sprung by the Radoslaw resistance group and one of the Panthers was set alight with Molotov cocktails. The crew escaped and boarded a second Panther, which turned into Mireckiego Street, where it in turn was hit with grenades, including either a British-made Gammon bomb or a PIAT projectile, which detonated behind the turret. During this attack, the Panther crashed into a house and both crews were taken prisoner. A third Panther, the last in the column, was immobilized with grenades on Okopowa Street, abandoned and captured intact.

The AK managed to hold the Wola area of Warsaw for a further 48 hours before two of

the tanks could be rendered operational. Two crews of six were picked from the most qualified members of the 'Zoska' battalion. A German POW was persuaded to help in the repair of the Panther named 'Pudel' by its new owners in honour of a fallen comrade. This tank was also named 'Magda' by its crew, a name with which it was immortalized. Magda was complete but required a fuel pump repair. A qualified Polish mechanic, who had been employed in the German tank maintenance facility, finally completed the repair on the evening of 3 August. The Panther was driven within sight of a German position a few streets away and the crew test-fired its main armament by firing until the German position was destroyed. The second Panther captured by the AK had been driven into a house during the ambush. This tank was freed by pulling down the dwelling in the process, after which it was inspected. Christened 'Felek', this slightly damaged Panther was also pressed into service.

Magda was sent into combat on 5 August in the operation planned to liberate the Saint Sofia hospital and destroy the KL Warschau concentration camp and the local police academy. Magda effectively supported the attack on the concentration camp, but the assaults on the hospital and the police academy were costly. Some 348 prisoners were released from the camp, some of whom joined the Zoska battalion to make up its losses. Felek was also employed in the police academy operation but was not as easily controlled through the action, arriving late and intervening only after heavy casualties, although the police academy eventually fell to the Home Army.

The two Panthers next saw action on 8 August supporting AK units fighting on Karolkowa Street. During this action, Magda sustained three 7.5cm hits from a German Panzer IV or Jagdpanzer 38t, wounding some of its crew. Two days later, Magda's crew destroyed two German armoured vehicles and enemy positions around the church of Saint Karol Boromeusz. Felek had by this time suffered severe mechanical problems, and after its ammunition was transferred to Magda it was blown up to prevent recapture. Magda remained operational until the next day, 11 August, when it was abandoned by its AK crew after being damaged in action.

During the Warsaw Uprising, the AK created a tank platoon organization named 'Wacek' from captured vehicles. It is a testament to the ingenuity of the small band of Armia Krajowa fighters who operated Felek, Magda, a Panzer

One of the most tragic episodes that occurred in World War II was the Warsaw Uprising. During the fighting between August and early October 1944, the Armia Krajowa captured a number of German tanks, including two operational Panthers. 'Pudel' (more commonly remembered as 'Magda') and 'Felek' (which is seen here), as the Panthers were named, were prominently marked with red and white markings on the front and sides. 'Felek' was more roughly marked than 'Magda', with large red and white markings on the turret sides and 'WP' (for 'Wojsko Polska', or 'Polish Army') very roughly painted in white on the turret rear hatch by its AK crew. (The Warsaw Uprising Museum)

'Dauphinée', one of two FFI-operated Panthers of the Escadron Besnier which participated in the siege and liberation of Royan in the spring of 1945. This Panther has been marked with a French *cocarde* on the side of its gun mounting, as well as with its *nom de baptême* – a practice observed by the FFI just as in the FFL. The name 'Chipie' painted in white on the barrel of the KwK 42 gun translates to 'rascal' or 'little devil'. (A. Beauvais, via L. Braeuer, Coll. Le Grand Blockhaus).

IV and several other captured AFVs that they succeeded in doing so with limited knowledge of operating tanks, without any supplies and with only meagre amounts of ammunition. One other captured Panther took part in a victory parade in Germany conducted by the Polish 1st Infantry Division 'Tadeusz Kościuszko' on 22 May 1945, but no record exists of its use in combat.

The Panther was known to the *Forces Françaises de l'Intérieur* (FFI, French resistance fighters) by the time of the Normandy landings, and FFI units encountered the Panther in combat in 1944 and 1945, amongst other German tank types. Without any capability of manufacturing tanks for themselves, the FFI still managed to salvage and repair captured enemy tanks from the multitude littering the French countryside as the Allies advanced out of Normandy. The FFI's *1er Groupe Mobile de Reconnaissance* (1er GMR, or 1st Mobile Reconnaissance Group) operated two Panthers under the command of Capitaine Guy Besnier. Besnier had prior armoured combat experience as a tank platoon commander in the 511e Régiment de Chars de Combat in 1940. The 1er GMR was formed from resistance personnel with prior experience in armoured units in the pre-war French Army. The 1er GMR was not tasked with a role in the advance eastward and was one of many resistance units that remained in western France awaiting incorporation into the FFL. Because equipment and the infrastructure to quickly add units to the FFL were not immediately available, FFI formations made do with a mixture of captured German weaponry. Most of its other equipment was a hodgepodge of gifted British and American uniforms and equipment, mixed with surviving 1940-era French *matériel*.

The 1er GMR was equipped with weaponry salvaged from the battlefield, with no supply chain to speak of. In the aftermath of the Normandy landings, Besnier's men were limited to hit-and-run operations conducted with captured German lorries on Wehrmacht units retreating eastwards. The 1er GMR was

B **POLISH HOME ARMY PANTHER AUSF Gs**

1. Panther Ausf G 'Magda'. The *Armia Krajowa*, or Home Army, captured three Panther Ausf Gs from the 19th Panzer Division in a single ambush sprung on Okopowa Street in proximity to Warsaw's Jewish cemetery on 2 August 1944. Two Panthers were repaired and put into use by the *Samodzielny Pluton Pancerny Batalionu Zośka* (Tank Platoon, Zośka Battalion), and were baptized 'Pudel' and 'Felek'. 'Pudel' was the more successfully employed of the two Home Army Panthers, becoming better known (unofficially) as 'Magda'. Its markings included British-style red–white–red identification markings on each side of the turret, a large Polish diced flag on the glacis, the stylized 'Wojska Polska' emblem next to it in white and the lily flower emblem of the Boy Scouts on the hull sides. The German *balkenkreuz* were carefully painted over with the red and white diced Polish emblem and the name 'Pudel' was painted on the right front mudguard.

2. Panther Ausf G 'Felek'. The second Panther, later named 'Felek', was hit by an anti-tank grenade on the turret rear during the 2 August 1944 ambush, and was driven into a house by its German crew before they fled. Felek has large 1919 white and red national flags roughly painted on each side of the turret. The rear of the turret is marked with a large brush-painted 'WP' for 'Wojska Polska' (Polish Army) in white paint. The standard *dunkel gelb* paint scheme and even the *balkenkreuz* on each side of the hull front remained throughout the Panther's brief career in the AK.

1

2

later tasked with static operations to contain the Germans encircled in the French Atlantic ports. It was here that Besnier's unit was able to ingeniously repair and then re-employ a whole range of vehicles driven away from where the enemy had abandoned them (due to fuel shortages or minor breakdowns).

Making tanks available for the 1er GMR through normal channels proved extremely difficult. The FFI lacked the political clout with the British and Americans enjoyed by the Forces Françaises Libres, and the 1er GMR had to rely on its own wits. In December 1944, Besnier found out that collection yards filled with captured German equipment had been assembled in Normandy, including tanks with minimal combat damage. Assembling a team of mechanically inclined FFI men and German POWs willing to collaborate, Besnier picked through several Normandy depots in December 1944.

The FFI scrounged through snowy salvage yards for enough armoured vehicles to create a credible squadron-sized armoured unit. This stood them in stark contrast to the FFL's two armoured divisions equipped from American stocks. The 1er GMR's German prisoners were mostly trained mechanics, who proved vital given the lack of technical documentation and maintenance facilities for tanks available to the FFI. In stark contrast to how the FFL's attempts to collect Panthers from American-controlled yards failed a few months later, the 1er GMR's men were apparently given access to the captured vehicles. Just how Besnier secured clearance to take the menagerie of tanks employed by the 1er GMR is not recorded, but he may have concentrated on securing these from 21st Army Group-controlled yards.

By the end of the month, the 1er GMR had taken over a Tiger Ausf E, a Panther Ausf A and a Panther Ausf G, 11 Panzer IVs, two Sturmgeschütz IIIs and a Jagdpanzer IV, supported by two FAMO Sdkfz 9 heavy recovery half-tracks. Given the problems with mechanical reliability that beset German units equipped with the Tiger and Panther, the achievement of the ad-hoc FFI mechanical staff (and their German collaborators) was noteworthy. The incredible luck of the 1er GMR was further borne out by the 300km road

C

FRENCH ARMY `DAUPHINÉ' AND `NORMANDIE'

1. 'Dauphiné'. The Forces Françaises de l'Interieur's 1er Groupe Mobile de Reconnaissance operated two Panthers amongst a mixed group of captured German tanks under the command of Captain Guy Besnier. All were rescued from assembly yards in the months that followed the Normandy breakout, and their careful repair by German prisoners culminated in early March 1945 when the unit was declared operational and renamed l'*Escadron Autonome de Chars Besnier* (Independent Armoured Squadron Besnier). They were ordered to move to the French Atlantic coast to invest the port of Royan. 'Dauphiné', seen here, was the better known of the squadron's two Panthers. Its markings include a French cockade applied on the gun trunnions, the vehicle name applied on a carefully scraped rectangle on each hull side and the nickname 'Chipie' on the gun barrel. The three-colour German camouflage scheme was retained until the war's end. 'Dauphiné' and its crew distinguished themselves in the liberation of Royan, and the Panther served in the 6e Regiment de Cuirassiers after the war.

2. 'Normandie'. The small number of Panthers operated by the French Army after the war spent much of their service in storage, but were also displayed publicly on several occasions. Between October 1949 and the end of 1952, 17 Panthers served in the *4e Escadron of the 503e Regiment de Chars de Combat* (or 4th Squadron of the 503e RCC). Most were named after French provinces, the names of which were painted on the turret sides (as we can see with 'Normandie' here). Each of the vehicles also bore a *numéro d'immatriculation* (which consisted of a black rectangle with white serial numbers and a small *tricolor* flag) applied on a scraped area on the glacis and on the lower part of the hull rear plate. All greasing points were painted red, and the exteriors of the vehicles were overpainted in two coats of olive drab-like *vert armée*. Most of these Panthers retained their original wartime zimmerit coating – often partly damaged. The vehicle interiors were repainted in an ivory 'cream' colour.

march successfully conducted by inexperienced drivers in winter conditions. They had moved the column from Normandy to the Royan area in south-west France, replenished with fuel and ammunition and with most of their tanks in some measure battleworthy.

In early March 1945, the 1er GMR was retitled the *Escadron Autonome de Chars Besnier* (Independent Armoured Squadron Besnier), and the unit prepared for combat operations on the Atlantic coast. The squadron first saw combat as an armoured unit two weeks later, on 15 March, during which the Panther Ausf G baptized 'Dauphiné' destroyed a German artillery observation position at a range of 3,500m. The same Panther was one of the first French tanks to penetrate the town of Royan at the end of the siege, but it never fought any duels against German tanks (which only made up a minor component of Royan's defences). Both Panthers remained operational throughout the siege and survived into the French Army's post-war inventory.

The FFL's relationship with their American allies grew acrimonious even before the final German surrender. One major knock-on effect was that the French Army enthusiastically embraced the plan to adopt the Panther as a potential supplement to the M4 medium tank in the *Arme Blindée Cavalerie* (Armoured Cavalry Arm). A second consequence was that the Americans frustrated French attempts to collect German equipment from areas that they controlled.

The British Army: 'Deserter' and 'Cuckoo'

The British Army faced the Panther in Italy and in North-West Europe in 1944 and 1945, but it was not dreaded to the same degree as the Tiger. The British QF 17-pdr gun of 1943 proved effective against the Panther at normal combat ranges, but these were not available in significant numbers as AFV-mounted weapon systems until mid-1944. The M10C tank destroyer, the Sherman Firefly and the less-successful Challenger A30 were all adaptations that served to get the 17-pdr into armoured and infantry divisions. None were as mobile or as well protected as the Panther. The total number of Panthers captured in running order with sufficient ammunition for combat use by Commonwealth forces in Italy and North-West Europe is not known, but probably amounted to tens of vehicles.

Only two captured Panthers were employed by British armoured regiments in combat, one each in Italy and in North-West Europe. In Italy, an early-production Panther Ausf A was evaluated by the Eighth Army in June 1944, but this vehicle was never turned upon its former owners and presumably succumbed to mechanical problems, leaving little trace other than a series of photos from late June 1944 (when it was employed to give rides to high-ranking officers, including General Sir Oliver Leese, commander of the Eighth Army). In contrast to the harsh evaluation of '433' in the summer of 1944, the Panthers used in combat by British crews during autumn 1944 and spring 1945 were highly regarded. The firepower, battlefield mobility and armour protection of the German tank were considered far better than the Sherman or Churchill. The performance on icy roads and in winter conditions of the Panther

The first British-captured Panther in Italy was a very early production Ausf A. It is seen here in late June 1944 being driven around with a number of highly ranked Eighth Army officers aboard, including their CO General Sir Oliver Leese. (IWM NA 15771)

the British named 'Cuckoo' was far better than the Churchills it served alongside. Panthers, *Bergepanthers* (armoured recovery vehicles) and *Jagdpanthers* (tank destroyers) were all considered to be of technical significance by the British, who also evaluated a *schmalturm* turret and the night vision devices intended for use with the Panthers at the end of the war.

The 21st Tank Brigade's 145th Battalion, Royal Armoured Corps (145th RAC) was gifted a Panther Ausf G by A Company, The Seaforth Highlanders of Canada (of the 2nd Infantry Brigade, 1st Canadian Infantry Division), which had been captured in a ditch near Martorano in northern Italy on 22 October 1944 during the advance to the Savio River. The capture followed an action in which the Seaforths' tank-hunting platoon destroyed several Panthers and self-propelled guns, winning one of its members a Victoria Cross. 'Popski's Private Army' (an irregular group of British Special Forces) seem to have laid a temporary first claim to this Panther, but eventually thought better of it. The Panther was thoroughly inspected, and after German explosives were removed and some missing gun components were replaced from a captured Pantherturm, the tank was rendered operational. Baptized 'Deserter', and carrying the markings of the Seaforths and the 145th RAC, the Panther was assigned to the latter's A Squadron. Its use in combat was brief, being used during a period of comparatively little tank vs tank action and primarily as a long-range precision artillery piece, destroying enemy observation posts in November 1944. After the 145th RAC was disbanded, 'Deserter' served as a demonstration vehicle to armoured units, and was later employed in mobility tests at Ravenna alongside Shermans and Churchills in March 1945. Problems with the Panther's transmission and a lack of spares eventually caused Deserter's abandonment, the tank having outlived its adoptive regiment by nearly four months. Its exact fate is unknown.

The second Panther (an Ausf G abandoned by 2.Abteilung, Panzerbrigade 107) was captured in working order by the 4th Battalion Coldstream Guards (6th Guards Tank Brigade) in the Dutch town of Overloon in late 1944. After a thorough examination and a coat of overall khaki drab paint, the tank was assigned to the regimental headquarters troop and was christened 'Cuckoo'. It was prominently marked with white stars to dissuade Allied air attack, but otherwise received no modifications. It was first used in

'Deserter' was a Panther Ausf G captured from Panzer Regiment 4, 26th Panzer Division by the Seaforth Highlanders of Canada in Italy on 22 October 1944. The tank, abandoned in running order but with one of the breech components removed, was made fully operational after some minor repairs. After passing interest in the machine from Popski's Private Army, it was taken into service by A Squadron, the 145th Battalion Royal Armoured Corps, 21st Tank Brigade, in November 1944. It first saw action on 11 November that year. (Tony Prentice, with thanks to Jeff Plowman)

D **'DESERTER', IN SERVICE WITH THE ROYAL ARMOURED CORPS, ITALY 1944/45**

The 21st Tank Brigade's 145th Battalion, Royal Armoured Corps (145th RAC) operated a Panther Ausf G captured in operational condition but with some of its breech components missing. The gun was repaired by the 145th RAC and the tank was named 'Deserter', joining A Squadron. The tank saw about two months of combat use in Italy's rainy winter of 1944/45, being employed largely as a mobile artillery system. The British crews of 'Deserter' were impressed by the Panther's firepower and mobility, even in muddy terrain. 'Deserter' was extensively marked by the 145th RAC: the Panther's glacis was adorned with the Seaforth Highlanders of Canada's and the 145th RAC's tactical symbols, and a prominent 21st Tank Brigade diabolo. All markings were applied over carefully scraped areas where the zimmerit had been removed. 'Deserter' appears to have been finished in German *dunkelgelb* overall, possibly with a light overspray of green or brown.

combat by the Coldstreams during the assault on the castle of Geijsteren on the Noord Brabant–Limburg border in the last week of November 1944. The castle's owner and a group of refugees fled the castle, which was occupied by Fallschirmjäger from Kampfgruppe Walther on 23 November, and the Coldstream Guards pounded the castle with 6-pdr, 75mm and 95mm gun fire from various marks of Churchill tank in between repeated air attacks.

The long 75mm gun of 'Cuckoo' proved a particularly accurate weapon, sending high explosive shells through the castle's windows with devastating effect. The castle was ruined in the attack, and Cuckoo proved a valuable prize. Ammunition supplies for 'Cuckoo' never posed any problems; it proved a superb gun platform and remained mechanically operational through nearly 90 days of operations (during which time maintenance was for the most part cursory). The 6th Guards Tank Brigade was next in action during Operation *Blackcock* in the second half of January 1945. This attack saw the British Second Army's 52nd Lowland and 43rd Wessex divisions attack through the Roermond–Sittard–Heinsberg area to secure the area east of the Roer River. Moving south of Venlo on the road towards Waldenrath, the Panther proved vastly superior on icy roads in comparison to the regiment's Churchills.

Like 'Deserter', 'Cuckoo' was never tested against German armour during its brief service with the British Army, but it was certainly the most extensively photographed and filmed of any of the Panthers captured by the Western Allies. The inevitable mechanical failure could not be staved off indefinitely, and around 22 February 1945, 'Cuckoo' broke down with a fuel pump failure east of Kleve during Operation *Veritable*. As spares were not available and the battalion was required to advance, the tank was simply abandoned where it had broken down. Less thoroughly documented captured Panther evidence exists in the Netherlands (where Free Polish troops captured an early-production Ausf D now preserved at Breda), but nowhere else were Panthers taken on strength in tank units or sent into combat against their former owners.

The FFL also operated a captured Panther in early 1945, some months after its 2e Division Blindée defeated an entire brigade of Panthers at Dompaire. In the aftermath of this battle, FFL officers were able to examine captured and destroyed Panthers in detail. Perhaps convinced by the 2e DB's accounts of the fighting against Panthers, the 5e Division Blindée's 1er Régiment de Chasseurs d'Afrique captured and rendered operational a broken-down Panther Ausf G of their own in March 1945 near Colmar. This tank (baptized 'Kaysersberg') was prepared by the regiment's Escadron D'Avout for use against its former owners in the advance into Germany. Repeated mechanical failures forced Kaysersberg's abandonment on 4 April before it could ever be used in battle. No other attempts by regular FFL units to operate Panthers were recorded during the war, perhaps because the FFL's

In order to avoid friendly fire, 'Deserter' was very prominently marked, which necessitated scraping off patches of its zimmerit anti-mine coating. During the reorganization of the Eighth Army's tank brigades in the winter of 1944/45, the 145th RAC was one of several infantry tank units that were broken up in order to provide reinforcements. 'Deserter' thereafter served in comparative trials with the Churchill and Sherman conducted by the Eighth Army. During its days with A Squadron, 145th RAC, it was well regarded and seems to have given no mechanical trouble. 'Deserter' was used in several demonstrations before the men of the Eighth Army (including New Zealand troops) in the province of Ravenna in March 1945 and was first employed in mobility trials on 22 December 1944, prior to the 145th RAC's dissolution. We can see the prominent markings applied on the left side of its turret. Amongst these, the call sign '10', the A Squadron triangle in yellow and '145 RAC' are visible. It does not appear that 'Deserter' was otherwise repainted, unlike 'Cuckoo'. In the spring of 1945, its transmission gave out while reversing during a demonstration, and from then its utility ended. It is possible that 'Deserter' was written off in mine trials because at least one photo exists of it stripped of tracks and suspension components. (Tony Prentice, with thanks to Jeff Plowman)

scarce resources and the pace of the advance in the spring of 1945 favoured the easier options available from the American supply chain.

PANTHERS IN POST-WAR SERVICE

The Soviet armies held by far the greatest stock of Panthers at the end of hostilities, but the actual number that could be rendered combat-worthy was very small. On 16 June 1945, the Red Army counted no fewer than 201 Panthers requiring repairs and only six operational Panthers in its inventory. Another 107 irreparably damaged vehicles were presumably also included in the inventory as a source of spare parts. A further 15 Jagdpanthers were listed in need of repair, and their post-war use appears to have been limited to trials. The captured Panthers were earmarked to partly equip the Bulgarian and Romanian armies as these changed sides towards the end of the war, but they were little used by the Red Army themselves (except as targets).

The remaining Panthers in Soviet hands after VE Day were stored, some eventually being transferred to several of the Eastern European armies as these 'declared themselves' for socialism. In Czechoslovakia and Poland, where wartime German maintenance centres had existed, several Panthers were collected by the Russians for potential future use.

Western intelligence reports identified inflated numbers of Panthers serving in the Czechoslovakian and Romanian armies until 1955, and certainly considered into the late 1940s that the Panther (and Tiger) might have been captured in sufficient numbers for regular post-war use as test

1

2

beds or as battle tanks in the Soviet Army. This could be the source of the perception in the West of entire units of Panthers in Red Army service. All evidence points towards perhaps three or four dozen operational Panthers and a smaller number of Bergepanthers selected to be put into first-line service between the armies of the Soviet allies Bulgaria, Romania and Czechoslovakia. Photographic evidence suggests that Poland employed a small number of Panthers post-war as training tanks, but must have done so only briefly. It is likely that examples in the USSR were stripped for parts, scrapped or expended as hard targets through the same period.

After the German surrender, one of the most unusual turns in the Panther story unfolded. This was the completion of a small evaluation series of nine Panthers and 12 Jagdpanthers by the British occupation forces in Hanover. These were manufactured by German workers under the supervision of Captain W. J. Hadlow and Corporal Bell of 823 Armoured Troops Workshops, Royal Electrical and Mechanical Engineers (REME). The Langenhagen and Maschinenfabrik Niedersachsen plants at Hanover-Linden, which manufactured both Panther Ausf G tanks and Jagdpanther tank destroyers, were taken over by the British. The gun factory at Laatzen was then returned to operation for finishing the partly built Panthers and Jagdpanthers from August 1945 until early 1946. This was achieved by rounding up former workers from the plants to clear bomb damage and the damaged machinery in both factories, and then employing them to complete the manufacturing process to original specification under British Army direction at Laatzen.

With a workspace cleared and with payment arranged through the local authorities, the plant's personnel built complete tanks from the basic chassis using up pre-cut plate and existing components. Component sourcing would have been impossible without the cooperation of factory foremen and other German craftsmen well acquainted with the logistics of Panther production in the Hanover area. The manufacturing work was completed without blueprints or manuals, a testament to the German workers' knowledge of their craft. Completed hulls were then tested without turrets (and without guns in the case of the Jagdpanthers). Turrets and weapons were sourced in turn, and all 21 vehicles were reputedly finished to production standard. Once completed and armed in the spring of 1946, examples of each type were sent to England for testing, the remainder being evaluated on Luneberg Heath for a short time by a special RAC detachment.

The results of troop testing of the 'British' Panthers and Jagdpanthers for crew ergonomics and tactical evaluation at Luneberg has left little trace thus far, but trials of the Panthers are believed to have been conducted by a special RAC detachment in 1946. Thereafter, records exist of some of these tanks being on firing ranges in Germany, presumably as catastrophic mechanical failures dictated. An unknown number of each type was, however, sent to Britain. Evaluation of two Jagdpanthers and

One of the Panthers assembled under British supervision undergoing evaluation on the former German training area at Putlos in the spring of 1946. The tests with the nine Panthers and 12 Jagdpanthers carried out after the war by the British Army were conducted in the UK as well as in Germany. After basic mobility trials proved impossible, several of the Panthers were used as targets in firing trials by the British Army in Germany. (The Tank Museum, Bovington)

two Panther Ausf Gs built under 823 Workshops' supervision was completed in 1948 at the Fighting Vehicles Proving Establishment in Chertsey, with a wartime Bergepanther (with 632km on the odometer) in attendance. The latter vehicle required a new engine installed prior to the trial.

If British evaluations of 1944 had been critical of the ergonomics and unreliability of the Panther '433', the more fulsome evaluation of the 823 Workshops' Panthers proved that all suffered from the mechanical fragility seen elsewhere with captured wartime

In French service the lower left corner of the front hull plate served as the location for the Panther's *numéro d'immatriculation* (registration number). Note that this tank does not carry a *nom de baptême*: vehicle names were generally painted on the turret sides following issue to units. (SHD – CAAPC Châtellerault)

Panthers. Issues with engine fires, brake failures and steering mechanism failures very quickly rendered several of the vehicles immobile. There were no spares provided, so the recovery vehicle was cannibalized for parts. The Panthers suffered so many mechanical failures that the report laconically summarized the whole fruitless endeavour as follows:

> Owing to the general mechanical unreliability of the Panther and Jagd Panther [*sic*] tanks insufficient test results have been obtained to allow any accurate assessment of the performance of these vehicles to be made.

After the evaluations were complete, some of the Panthers and Jagdpanthers were presumably repaired, as Jagdpanthers were reportedly used as extemporized towing vehicles on experimental establishments and subsequently as hard targets in Britain. No specific information regarding Jagdpanther trials by the Royal Artillery or RAC has yet been found. A pristine example of an 823 Workshops Panther Ausf G and a Jagdpanther were preserved in the Bovington Tank Museum collection. Amazingly, several other of the 823 Workshops' Panthers were later recovered from firing ranges and scrapyards and were restored by other museums.

Panthers were used as hard targets for gun development as late as 20 June 1949, when an Ausf A was used to compare the armour-penetrating capabilities of the 32-pdr and 20-pdr guns fitted to the A39 Tortoise heavy assault tank and a Centurion Mk 3. Some of the Panthers and Jagdpanthers produced for the 823 Workshops were also used as hard targets for British gunnery trials in Germany.

Bulgaria

In early 1945, the 1st Tank Battalion of the First Bulgarian Army was formed and incorporated into the Red Army's 3rd Ukrainian Front. All the vehicles to equip the battalion were delivered to the Bulgarians from German tanks captured in the 3rd Ukrainian Front's sector in January 1945. On 17 March 1945, the first Panther was received for the battalion's heavy tank company. Delays ensued and the crews assigned to the 1st Tank Battalion only received their remaining 14 Panthers at Pana Deveger in Hungary on 14 April. Crew training started immediately under the supervision of Soviet instructors, but there was no hope of action before the war was over.

At the end of May 1945, the Panthers were entrained for Sofia. On 1 March 1946, there were 15 Panthers in service in the 1st Tank Company, all but one of which were nominally operational. It appears that the vehicles were kept on strength until the 1950s but in deep reserve, so we can imagine that they saw little use. As Soviet equipment was made available in the early 1950s, the Panthers became surplus to requirements and they were probably scrapped at this time. It is possible that some were dug in as fortifications at strategic points along Bulgaria's mountainous border with Greece, but none have survived.

A Romanian T-5 (here based on a Panther Ausf D), seen in 1946. Between the end of the war and 1947, Romania remained a monarchy, and the T-5s received from the USSR were prominently marked with the St Michael's cross in yellow, red and blue, surmounted with the royal crown. In December 1947, Romania became a socialist republic and the markings were changed to a simple disc with the Romanian tricolour inscribed 'RPR', the standard national marking retained until 1951. In that year, a blue-bordered yellow roundel with a five-pointed red star inscribed 'RPR' was adopted in its place. The T-5s then served in the Tudor Vladimirescu-Debrecin Armoured Division. (Fond Dubarry, Collection du Musée des Blindés de Saumur)

Romania

The Panther was never provided to Romania by its German ally prior to the country going over to the Allied side, but the USSR supplied Panthers to the Romanian Army from captured stocks during the war. On 15 January 1945, the Romanian 1st Armoured Regiment and 2nd Armoured Regiment were assigned to the 1st Armoured Brigade. Equipment included captured late-model Panzer IVs (designated T-4) and Panthers (Ausf D, A and G, all of which were designated T-5). Use of the Romanian T-5s in combat against the Germans is not recorded, but the type remained in service after the war.

By agreement with the Soviet government, an unknown number of Panthers from Red Army stocks were transferred to the Romanian Army after the war. These were to be employed in a single heavy tank company in the 1st Armoured Brigade. During 1947, the brigade was dissolved and its elements were reorganized into elements of the Tudor Vladimirescu-Debreţin Armoured Division and the Horea, Cloşca şi Crişan Mechanized Division. Both of these divisions were raised from Romanian wartime prisoners of war in the USSR who were willing to prove their dedication to socialism. On 1 May 1949, the two new divisions were formed into a mechanized corps, which was completely re-equipped with Soviet armoured vehicles during the course of 1950. The T-5s were then placed into storage as war reserves, being reportedly scrapped after 1955.

Czechoslovakia

Hundreds of Panthers were recuperated on Czechoslovak territory after the

F

BULGARIAN ARMY T-5s

1. In Bulgarian service the Panther was designated T-5, the first of which were received after the Bulgarian Army changed sides in March 1945. Here we can see a T-5 battle tank of the 1st Company, 1st Tank Battalion in March 1946. Fifteen T-5s (including examples of all three models) were employed by the Bulgarian Army between April 1945 and the early 1950s, before replacement with T-34-85s. These tanks were painted olive green and were marked with large red stars on the turret sides.

2. After the T-5s were retired in the early 1950s, some of these tanks were emplaced as frontier fortifications (along with some Panzer IVs) at strategic points on the Bulgarian–Greek border. It is likely that the Bulgarian T-5s spent most of their service in reserve or in storage due to the shortage of available spares.

1

2

The post-war Czechoslovakian Army, in a similar manner to the French Army, made extensive plans to take the Panther into service. It was designated T-42/75, but just as in France, getting the Panther into service (even with a substantial refurbishment programme) was problematic. Some of the Panthers collected after the war for further service were handed over to the Czechoslovak authorities from stocks captured on Czechoslovakian territory by the Red Army. This T-42/75 was photographed on the firing ranges at Vyškov, and this image is believed to date from around 1950. The exterior stowage mountings have been removed, which may indicate that this tank was stripped for parts to keep others in service. The remains of a large circular marking are visible on the turret side. Fewer than 40 T-42/75s were rendered operable (all apparently Ausf Gs), and after comparatively brief use, most were stored and later scrapped. Fifteen were converted into unarmed recovery tractors. (Collection Bohumír Kudlička)

war, and approximately 60 of those deemed repairable were stocked in 1947. A small number of these were employed as training vehicles at the Czechoslovak Tank School. Eventually, over 50 Panther and Bergepanther chassis received Czechoslovakian serial numbers. One of the uses considered for the Panther by the Czechoslovak general staff in 1946/47 was as a chassis for self-propelled gun designs. The Panther was proposed as a chassis for PaK 43 88mm anti-tank guns and for field (105mm), medium (152mm) and heavy (305mm) artillery systems with four-man crews. The anti-tank version was never completed, but the self-propelled medium artillery systems were intended to be armed with sFH 15cm guns, rebored to fire Soviet 152mm ammunition (and redesignated 152.4mm No18/47 N in Czechoslovakian service).

A design project for the chassis portion was undertaken by Škoda, who had examined such a project on their own initiative during 1946. Škoda is believed to have been loaned a Panther Ausf D (possibly chassis number 213083) in March 1947 to work out the drawings and layout for the gun mounting. In June of that year, Škoda and the VTU military technical institute at Plzeň were asked to design two 46-ton prototypes. Drawings for two self-propelled gun configurations (designated 16057P and 16058P) were completed in July 1947, but it is unknown if either proposal was completed or if trials were conducted.

A self-propelled field gun proposal followed in August 1947, designated the

G   CZECHOSLOVAKIAN ARMY VT-42 AND HUNGARIAN ARMY AUSF D

1. The Czechoslovakian Army intended to render 40 T-42/75 heavy tanks and 14 VT-42 recovery vehicles operational from the stock of captured Panthers and variants they held in 1948. These targets slipped in 1949 and again in 1950, by which time the possibility of adopting Panthers as T-42/75 heavy tanks in any capacity other than as limited-standard training vehicles evaporated. CKD and Škoda both lent their expertise to the refurbishment programme, but in the end only 32 T-42/75 Panther tanks and 12 VT-42s were completed for the Czechoslovakian Army. Unlike the T-42/75s (which went into storage as war reserves in Milovice, Dědice and Martin), the VT-42 recovery vehicle saw more consistent use. The operable T-42/75s in storage were converted into recovery tractors or scrapped after 1952, when the Soviets allowed license production of the T-34-85 in Martin. The VT-42s were painted in overall olive green, and some were marked with large hull numbers in white on the hull sides in service.

2. Hungary was the only one of Germany's Axis allies to employ the Panther in combat, although Romania had attempted unsuccessfully to order Panthers prior to its defection to the Allies in 1944. While most of the relatively few surviving photographs of Panthers in Hungarian service show later vehicles, this Ausf D served with the 2nd Armoured Division in late 1944. The paint scheme is simply overall German *dunkelgelb* with large '222' turret numbers applied in white. The German *balkenkreuz* on the hull side may have been repainted with an early-pattern Hungarian cross, and the vehicle is believed to have been coated with zimmerit, which may indicate a rebuilt example of an early D.

1

2

ShK-Panther, which mounted a captured German 10.5cm sK 18 gun (designated 105mm vz.18 N in Czechoslovak service). No prototypes were known to have been completed. A third class of Panther-based artillery system was proposed by Škoda in late 1946, this time a heavily modified Panther hull to carry the 305mm B20 heavy mortar, designated TShM-Panther. This design required the hull side armour to be substantially removed to stay within practical weight limits. Ammunition stowage on board the vehicle for the 305mm rounds would have been problematic, but might have been located on a platform over the engine decks. Drawings Zb 16053-P and Zb 16054-P were prepared for the massive self-propelled mortar, but like the two lighter artillery self-propelled guns, resources were not available in post-war Czechoslovakia for series production.

In October 1948, the decision was made to repair 40 Panthers as T-42/75 heavy tanks and 14 Bergepanthers as T-42 recovery vehicles. CKD and Škoda were brought into the refurbishment programme due to the experience and facilities available in both companies. The ČKD plant in Prague and the Škoda company in Plzeň were both included in overhauling 30 T-42/75s and 14 T-42 recovery vehicles from 14 January 1949. It was expected that the last ten T-42/75s could be completed in 1950. However, the programme objectives proved overly optimistic because of component shortages, and in 1950 the Czechoslovak Army re-evaluated the situation. It was then decided that only 32 T-42/75 Panther tanks and 12 T-42 recovery vehicles could be reworked.

By the end of the year, the VT-42 recovery vehicles had been refurbished and issued to the Czechoslovak Army. The T-42/75 Panthers were then issued to the army, but these immediately went into storage as war reserves (with turrets reportedly dismounted and stored in a separate warehouse in Milovice). The remaining Panther hulks assembled in Milovice were cannibalized for spare parts, and then scrapped (or used as targets). In April 1952, Panthers were in storage at Dědice (near Vyškov), Martin and Žilina. Efforts to set up a production line for spares at Brno were erroneously recounted in CIA reports during the same period. All of the Czechoslovak Army's T-42/75 tanks were eventually handed over to the 1st Heavy Tank and Self-Propelled Regiment in Strašice. These saw limited use in training alongside the regiment's ISU-152s and IS-2s. After T-34-85 production started at Martin, 15 T-42/75s were converted into unarmed recovery tractors in 1955 and the rest were eventually scrapped. By the time the T-42/75 was retired in 1959, seven T-42 recovery tanks and 15 T-42/75s converted into recovery tractors remained in the army's inventory.

One Bergepanther was fitted with the T-34/85's V12 diesel engine in the 1950s to determine options to prolong the life of these useful vehicles. At least one of the Czechoslovak Army's Bergepanthers was later employed as a civil heavy construction and recovery vehicle into the 1960s. The Czechoslovakian T-42/75s and T-42 recovery tanks were reportedly painted in overall dark green and retained their Wehrmacht-era tools and fittings. It is interesting to note that Western intelligence service reports on the Czechoslovak Army's efforts to refurbish their Panthers overestimated the programme's limited success. The T-42/75's service life appears to have consisted of brief use as training vehicles followed by storage, while T-34-85 production got off the ground at Martin. The T-42 recovery vehicle saw more effective use through the 1950s, a time when the Czechoslovak Army re-equipped extensively with Soviet armoured vehicles.

The French Army

The Forces Françaises Libres captured the first Panther to be locally examined by Allied forces in Italy in March 1943. The obvious quality of the design and possibility of France holding a considerable stock of captured German Panthers at the war's end generated an enormous amount of wishful thinking regarding post-war equipment with the type in the FFL. The realities were very different. As soon as Paris was liberated in late August 1944, France began the struggle to rearm itself by its own means where possible. Some pre-war French weapons resumed limited production, and the use of captured German equipment in the French Army became common (notably as resistance units were integrated into the FFL). Tanks had not been manufactured substantially in France during the occupation, and pre-war facilities were so heavily damaged as to render tank manufacture impossible after the liberation. Most of the pre-war armoured vehicle production sites and arsenals had served as maintenance facilities during the occupation but suffered wholesale sabotage prior to the Wehrmacht's departure. French attempts to adopt the Panther as a standard tank type came as disillusion took hold at France's subordinate place in the post-war Western alliance.

The lack of spares available was always the single greatest obstacle to using captured Panthers in wartime. The Panther's post-war use was rendered problematic by the very same issue. Nonetheless, the French Army fielded the Panther as a limited standard weapon while its own defence industry was rebuilt after the war, becoming the only army in Western Europe to adopt the type. Panthers figured amongst a substantial variety of captured German armoured vehicles rendered serviceable by French arsenals for temporary use (or for sale abroad) in the late 1940s.

A scene from the liberation of Paris in 1944? Well, actually no, this is a movie set *circa* June 1947 which featured two of the French Army's reconditioned Panthers rolling along by the Préfecture de Police on the Île de la Cité. The film, now long-forgotten by most, was *Un flic et la 2ème DB* by Maurice Decarange. (N. Couderc)

The Panthers assembled in 1945 in France formed the nucleus of what was hoped might amount to several battalions. On 8 June 1945, the FFI's Escadron Besnier was incorporated into the regular French Army, becoming the 6e Régiment de Cuirassiers' (6e RC) second squadron. The regiment was

This rebuilt Panther Ausf A was photographed at Gien, and we can see that the new coat of *vert armée* has failed to totally cover the old *balkankreuz* marking from its previous Wehrmacht owners. (SHD – CAAPC Châtellerault)

assigned to the French forces tasked with occupation duties in Western Germany, retaining its hodgepodge of captured German equipment (including both Panthers). Six other Panthers recovered from across occupied France were added to the unit's inventory before the year's end. When the 6e RC was disbanded in March 1946, a substantial amount of experience had been accumulated in operating the Panther, which was documented. The regiment's equipment was transferred into reserve at Gien (the French Army's central workshops) during the following month.

The French high command prioritized using German equipment as an official policy in 1945, known as 'Programme D'. There was at the time no shortage of abandoned German equipment littering the French landscape. Depots of captured tanks were present in Lorraine, where hundreds of Panthers were lost in action. Many of these Panthers were evaluated for restoration to a serviceable condition (or were cannibalized for parts) by the French Army. French aspirations to adopt the Panther into their own army faced several hurdles, the first of which was Supreme Headquarters Allied Expeditionary Force (SHAEF) control over many of the captured vehicle dumps. The relationship between SHAEF and the FFL's leadership was by then acrimonious. On 14 June 1945, SHAEF announced its intention to destroy or demilitarize all captured AFVs in its weapons dumps. This order excluded any vehicles useful to British and American research, but denied the possibility of securing repairable Panthers for the French. The total number of Panthers available to the French could now be counted only in tens rather than in hundreds, as had been hoped for. Moreover, many of these had been abandoned due to mechanical failure rather than from combat damage: assembling and repairing the Panthers for further service proved a terribly difficult task in the chaotic conditions that followed France's liberation.

The surviving evidence indicates that only 41 Panther Ausf As and Gs were recovered in undamaged or repairable condition by the French Army. These were assembled and delivered to AMX between the end of 1945 and 1950. A further 18 Panthers, judged suitable for cannibalization, were sent to AMX in the same period. Once most of these tanks were stripped of

H **ROMANIAN PANTHER T-5 AUSF. D**

Romania's Panthers were supplied from Russian stocks in early 1945 and included D, A and G models, all of which shared the designation T-5. These were augmented after the war with Soviet-supplied Panthers for use in a single heavy tank company in the 1st Armoured Brigade. In 1947, this company was incorporated into the Tudor Vladimirescu-Debreţin Armoured Division, where it served until 1950. The T-5s were placed in reserve when Soviet tanks were received by Romania. The Romanian tank markings worn on T-5s in 1946 included the Royal Romanian Army's cross of St Michael surmounted by a royal crown, the basic vehicle colour being the wartime German *dunkelgelb* that the vehicles were presumably delivered in. These markings were discontinued in 1948 after the socialist People's Republic of Romania deposed the king, being replaced with a vertically divided Romanian tricolour insignia marked 'RPR'. All the Romanian Panthers were scrapped in the mid-1950s.

1

2

Sweden's army had expressed an interest in the Panther ever since 1943, but only acquired one after the war. A Panther Ausf A was provided by the French government, and was preserved in the Swedish Army's technical collection. The distinctive rungs welded onto the glacis permitted easier mounting for the crew. It is seen without its muzzle brake in this photo. A second modification added in Sweden were the headlamps and brushguards seen here. Whilst a Tiger Ausf B acquired by the Swedish Army in the same period was shot to pieces on the firing ranges following evaluation, the Panther appears to have been maintained in running condition for several years. The Panther evaluated in Sweden was presented to the Bundeswehr in good condition in 1960, and survives in the museum at Munster. (National War Archive of Sweden)

The AMX facility at Satory was the scene of several trials with the French Army's Panthers by DEFA, and two were retained on site permanently in the years after the war. This trial was set up to test out the suspension and track's characteristics with the first road wheel removed. (Fond Dubarry, Collection du Musée des Blindés de Saumur)

useful components, 15 were expended as hard targets for specific gunnery tests, one was sent to the FCM workshops as a reference vehicle and another was retained for display at Saumur. The vehicle identified for preservation at Saumur is one of the three still existing in the museum's collection.

During the war, Swedish interest in the Panther was expressed to the Germans, but only after the war were attempts to secure a Panther (from the French government) successful. In mid-1946, a Swedish delegation travelled to France and looked over several captured Panthers at AMX at Satory, selecting a Panther Ausf A (chassis number 210767) for shipment to Sweden. It is unclear whether the vehicle was sold or gifted to the Swedes, but the tank was shipped to Rouen shortly thereafter and arrived in Sweden for evaluation in the middle of 1947. Following a long technical evaluation, which included extensive mobility trials, the Panther was preserved in the Swedish Army's technical collection. It was presented to West Germany for the armour collection at the Bundeswehr's Panzertruppenschule I at Munster in 1960.

Eight Panthers were serving in Germany with the 6e RC before the end of 1945, 13 more were placed into storage at Gien at the beginning of 1946 and one was sent to the central gunnery establishment at Bourges (ETBS, *Établissement Technique de Bourges*). Seventeen Panthers were issued to the 503e Régiment de Chars de Combat at Mourmelon in 1949/50 (including some of those previously used by the 6e RC). Two Panthers were kept at AMX in Satory as reference vehicles. The two Panthers parked in front of Les Invalides to commemorate the 2e Division Blindée and four Jagdpanthers used in technical trials were not included in these totals. Forty-one Panthers weren't enough to equip a full battalion, and the total number was never concentrated for a variety of reasons. Spares were very hard to accumulate, which may seem strange for a

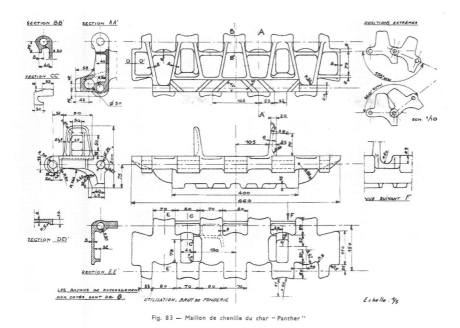

Fig. 83 — Maillon de chenille du char " Panther "

Like the Red Army, the French Army also produced a detailed technical manual, most of which was translated from German technical literature. Missing portions of the relevant documentation were, however, reverse-engineered, presumably with German help after the war. The creation of technical documentation for the maintenance and use of the Panther by the French Army was accomplished simultaneously to the inspection and renovation programme carried out by DEFA. (SHD - CAAPC Châtellerault)

country with entire stockyards filled with wartime wrecks awaiting the cutting torch, but often these extended to less durable components like gears, gaskets and seals (which were not easily recycled).

The French Army's Panthers needed a factory overhaul, and technical documentation for them was translated or reverse-engineered by the French themselves. Crew training and the accumulation of an adequate store of ammunition were other problems navigated as the Panther was introduced into French service after the war. The French Army's resources (as well as those of DEFA, the government's central armaments administration) were extremely meagre in 1945. Priorities were divided between the war in Indochina, DEFA programmes like the ARL 44 and AMX 50 M4 tanks, and the rehabilitation of weapons manufacturing capability. Sustaining the Panthers soon dropped to the bottom of the list, becoming a matter of crawling through scrapyards for

Given the *immatriculation* 1004729 and operated here without its turret fitted, this is a second photo of the shortened suspension trial. The Panther's suspension and track system (along with that employed on the Tiger *Ausfuhrung* B) were studied closely by AMX and influenced the development of suspension systems adopted on France's AMX 50 M4. (Fond Dubarry, Collection du Musée des Blindés de Saumur)

parts and attempting to trace component manufacturers in occupied Germany.

DEFA assigned AMX (*Ateliers d'Issy les Moulineaux at Satory*) the responsibility for refurbishing the Panther hulls, giving APX (Ateliers de Puteaux) responsibility for the turrets. Problems quickly piled up, despite the inclusion of captured German maintenance staff in both projects. Besides the doubtful mechanical condition of the captured Panthers, outdoor storage and general neglect had also taken their toll. Late-production Panthers were poorly made compared to the early models, and all were dependent on regular maintenance in order to remain operational. A report in the 6e RC's regimental notes dated 31 January 1946 records the warnings to his French captors of a German POW 'instructor' then serving to help train Panther drivers:

> The first Panthers were very well built, but little by little the quality of components dropped. An advantage of the early models was very precise steering, but after 250 to 300 kilometers of operation, an engine change was normally necessary. [On this issue the driver was most likely describing the removal and inspection of the engine per manufacturer's maintenance recommendations.] Engine and transmission bearings and cylinder heads were weak points. A 100 km drive on the tank's tracks was exceptional without prolonged maintenance so we minimized track mileage unless it was for approach marches or for actual combat.

The 6e RC soon discovered that the Panther's other great weakness was its fragile final drives. Earlier road tests made in July 1945 by DEFA engineers noted:

> [W]hile the Panther could attain a speed of 55 kilometers an hour (with the engine running at 3,000 RPM) on a good road, this speed could not be maintained and was detrimental to the drivetrain's components. The suspension lasted 2,000km–3,000km before components began to fail (versus the designed life cycle of 5,000 km). The gearboxes lasted for an average of 9,000 km, but the weak point of the suspension were [*sic*] the steering brakes – which were prone to failure, resulting in a recommended speed limit of 40 km per hour. It was quite apparent that the machine had been rushed into production without enough time to resolve these problems.

By 14 September 1945, a large stock of 75mm ammunition for the KwK 42 was gathered for inspection and stocking at the Arsenal de Bourges, France's premier artillery complex. The 6e RC provided four of its eight operational Panthers for a series of range tests. The vehicles involved were 'Lorraine' (*immatriculation* 1004703), 'Bretagne' (*immatriculation* 1004718), 'Picardie' (*immatriculation* 1004705) and 'Auvergne' (*immatriculation* 1004711). Each was provided with ten rounds of high-explosive shell, and by the end of the trial no fewer than five misfires had occurred. The trial was judged a success insofar as the guns had functioned perfectly, but the storage conditions for the captured ammunition stock were reviewed and an inspection programme was rapidly put into place.

In 1947, a report on the Panther as a weapon system was completed by the Section Technique de l'Armée (STA). The Panther was evaluated for its perceived weaknesses as well as its evident strengths. The 75mm KwK 42 in particular was recognized for its good overall design and the quality of its Pz.Gr 39/42 and Pz.Gr 40 armour-piercing and high-explosive munitions. A noted exception was the gun's recoil system, which was not sufficiently robust for prolonged rapid-fire engagements of over 20 rounds. Praise for the Panther's firepower was tempered by many criticisms regarding the turret systems. The report noted: 'The turret traverse drive is not strong enough to either turn the turret or hold it in place when the Panther is on an incline of more than 20 degrees. The Panther is therefore not capable of firing when driving cross-country.' It went on to note that without pneumatic elevation assist, the gun was poorly balanced and difficult to elevate. Nonetheless, the Panther was described as an excellent gun platform. The excellent vision from the commander's cupola was tempered by the gunner's lack of vision devices other than his periscopic sight. This factor was believed to contribute to a lower overall degree of situational awareness and slower engagement times than was possible for the crew in an M4-series medium tank.

The front of the former FFI Panther carries the *tricolor* painted on the glacis- and externally (at least) the vehicle appears very complete. This of course was no assurance of the vehicle's combat worthiness. The AMX facility was tasked with inspecting each of these vehicles, which came from battlefields all over northern and eastern France. Many of the Panthers inspected by AMX had damaged or misaligned optics and had suffered over a year of exposure and neglect. The special commission set up to rehabilitate a useful number of these vehicles was able to systematically identify assemblies that required repair or replacement. (SHD – CAAPC Châtellerault)

Although not yet wearing its French army *immatriculation*, this Panther was one of those overhauled for further service. This picture dates from late 1945 or early 1946 and was taken at Billancourt, in one of the Renault factories. Its presence there is a mystery, because Renault was not involved with any of the programmes to inspect or overhaul the Panthers as French army equipment after the war. It is possible that it was on the premises for temporary storage. (Fond Dubarry, Collection du Musée des Blindés de Saumur)

The 'Normandie' seen here was amongst the Panthers operated by the 6e *Régiment de Cuirassiers* (6e RC) in July 1945. These tanks were completed from available spares, repainted in vert armée and received their army *immatriculation* (in this case number 1004701). In 1949 these tanks were then passed on to the *503e Régiment de Chars de Combat*. The Panthers were amongst the most powerful tanks in the French inventory, but by then they were admittedly a stop gap while more modern vehicles were designed and tested. (SHD – CAAPC Châtellerault)

A Panther receiving committee was assembled at the same time to outline the specific testing required prior to the issue of each rebuilt tank. By 2 June 1949, the Panthers accepted for the French Army from DEFA's facilities were given the requirement of passing the same kind of testing applied to newly manufactured armoured vehicles. A battery of tests was conducted to prove both the hull and turret systems. These included a 45-minute drive test (including 15 minutes over rough terrain), a 45km/h speed test on roads and a brake test conducted on a 60 per cent gradient travelling both up and down. Perhaps most notable was a neutral turn test. The turret had to rotate a full turn in 17 seconds with the engine turning at 2,500rpm and in 45 seconds with the engine at 2,000rpm. Traverse tests were conducted to ensure that targets could be acquired and tracked. All greasing points were painted red and all moving parts were tested to ensure that the vehicle's regulatory 'two coats of olive green on the vehicle exterior and two coats of cream paint on its interior' caused no obstruction or sticking. Testing of the gun was also outlined in detail. Each 75mm gun was fired at 0 degrees elevation to warm the chamber and barrel, followed by three to five 7.5cm Pz.Gr.Patr 39/42 KwK rounds to ensure that the gun breech and associated equipment were in adequate condition.

The degree of attention given to each of the tanks was exceptional for a reconditioned weapon only available in tiny quantities. This reflected the Panther's perceived combat value at a time when DEFA's development of new French battle tanks was constantly falling behind schedule. Getting

'Normandie' was not quite complete, however, as we can see here in July 1945– the lid on the right rear stowage bin is missing. The 6e RC was the heir to the wartime FFI's *Escadron Besnier*, and it operated eight Panthers as part of its equipment. These photos were taken when some of the 6e RC's Panthers were used in firing trials at Bourges, alongside a StuG III, to test out the characteristics of different 75mm rifled guns. The trials in question were held at Bourges because the *Atelier de Puteaux* lacked the necessary facilities at this time. (SHD - CAAPC Châtellerault)

the reconditioned Panthers into an operational state was a painfully slow process, at a time when the French Army was suffering acute shortages of *matériel* and manpower. The committee's 5 August 1949 recommendation to the secretary of the army underlined the spares shortage, warning that the Panthers should only be used as training vehicles until new tanks were brought into service. These 'new tanks' were a reference to the ARL 44 and the more advanced AMX 50 M4 prototype then both under evaluation.

Two Panthers recovered from the battlefield at Dompaire stood guard for many years at the north entrance of *Les Invalides*. Neither of these two tanks were good enough for reconditioning. (Fond Dubarry, Collection du Musée des Blindés de Saumur)

Between October 1949 and February 1950, the 4e Escadron of the 503e Régiment de Chars de Combat (or 4th squadron of the 503e RCC, which had been raised from the dissolved 6e RC) was slowly issued 17 of the reconditioned Panthers. Prior to issue, each vehicle's wireless equipment was carefully tested. The total issue was shipped in three lots of four Panthers, with a final shipment of five vehicles, each transported on ex-Reichsbahn tank cars with only 200 litres of fuel in the tanks. All optics, stowage and machine guns were removed. AMX was responsible for supplying a separate shipment with a nominal quantity of spares for each vehicle.

By early 1950, it is reasonably assumed that the 17 Panthers issued to the 503e RCC were the very best of the 41 vehicles available in France, and that all of the remainder by then served as a source of vehicle spares. AMX's records for the period conceded that few of the available spares were in fact new parts. This situation limited the availability of replacement vehicles and the service life of the French Panthers. The Panthers served alongside ARL 44s from early 1951 to late 1952, but the regiment had limited use of its tanks due to spares and breakdowns, amongst other problems. AMX conceded that the principal value of Panthers was as temporary training vehicles until something better came along – although the army had to wait until 1952 when these arrived as MAP M26s and M47s. Once the M26

Some of the Panthers collected by the French army were used for weapons tests. This Ausfuhrung G named 'Le Buffle' was used for mine trials, as we can deduce by the state of its suspension. (SHD - CAAPC Châtellerault)

and M47 became available, the Panthers became surplus to requirements. Unsubstantiated rumours have persisted to the present time of at least one Panther being tested in Indochina, but no archival material to support this was uncovered in the research for this book. Efforts to sell refurbished Panthers to Syria appear to have been reported by the CIA in the 1950s, but these were probably erroneous (likely being confused with Panzer IV medium tanks and Sturmgeschütz III assault guns sold to Syria by both France and Czechoslovakia).

We must recognize that in French service, the Panthers spent much of their time undergoing maintenance or in storage – and never proved themselves as satisfactory combat vehicles. By the time the Panther was withdrawn in late 1952, only ten of the 503e RCC's vehicles were still operational, which actually compared favourably with the number of contemporary ARL 44 tanks laboriously built by DEFA after the war. The Panthers were at the end of their mechanical lives by this point. With hindsight, the decision to proceed with adopting Panthers into French service after it became obvious that the Americans would never release the Panthers in their custody in 1945 stands out as an impractical measure – seen to fruition as a matter of national pride. It reflected a larger national determination to act independently in military matters without foreign interference, as was visible in other French policies followed in the same period.

THE PANTHER AS A TEMPLATE

Hungary's wartime 44M tank design was directly influenced by the Panther, although none were actually built. The Panther's contribution to French tank design in the immediate post-war period deserves examination. The Panther's 75mm gun was deemed an ideal high-velocity gun for light and medium tanks. The DEFA CN-75-50 75mm gun used in the AMX 13 took the 75mm KwK 42's barrel as its starting point, while the German gun's ammunition types were evaluated extensively in the development of French high-velocity anti-tank rounds. The CN-75-50 went on to arm the AMX 13 Mle 51, and the same gun was produced by DEFA as a kit to up-gun Sherman tanks employed by Israel and India.

Amazingly, AMX spent considerable efforts developing the Panther's ZF AK-7-200 transmission, which had proven so troublesome in German service. The Panther's Maybach HL230 engine and ZL transmission were used in modified form in the French ARL 44 Char de Transition, adopted in 1950 and used alongside the Panther in the 503e RCC. The basic layout of the Panther's hull was considered closely in the development of the

Without doubt seen at the AMX facility, this is a Panther photographed next to a diminutive AMX prototype then designated 'Char de 12 Tonnes' –- which was developed into the AMX 13. The two shared a certain commonality, for the KwK 42 7.5cm gun that armed the Panther was taken as the starting point for the Canon 75mm Mle 1950 that went on to arm the AMX 13 Mle 51. AMX also drew inspiration from the Panther's transmission as the starting point for the type that was eventually employed in the AMX 30B. (SHD – CAAPC Châtellerault)

AMX 50 M4 medium tank and for the AMX 50 120 heavy tanks evaluated between 1949 and 1958. An important DEFA improvement to their own interpretation of the Panther's layout was a rear-mounted transmission and final drive. Elements of the running gear, sprocket and tracks were copied extensively from the Panther. The Tiger B's Maybach HL295 provided the powerplant for the AMX 50 prototypes, but like the Panther from which it drew much of its inspiration, the AMX 50 never really achieved the balance of mobility and reliability the French Army desired. Nonetheless, the experience of operating the Panther and the study of its design taught DEFA much about tank design – which went on to benefit France's first main battle tank, the AMX 30.

BIBLIOGRAPHY AND SOURCES

Russian sources

Samsonov, Peter, 'Captured Tanks in the Red Army', www.tankarchives.ca (2 March 2014 and 4 July 2016)

Samsonov, Peter, 'None More Frightening Than the Cat', www.tankarchives.ca (11 May 2019)

Samsonov, Peter, 'Panther Trials', www.tankarchives.ca (8 April 2014)

Samsonov, Peter, 'Valentines and Panthers', www.tankarchives.ca (9 October 2013)

T-V Pantera, Technical Manual (Moscow, 1944)

CIA reports

CIA RDP82-00457R000800210004-0, 'German Weapons in Use by the Soviet Army' (19 August 1947)

Polish sources

Ledwoch, J., *PzKpfw V Sd Kfz 171 'Panther'* (Czesc I)

British sources

55/534/9/2 (AFV Technical Reports ME), Italy (1945)

'Armour Branch Report on Comprehensive Firing Trials against German Panther Pz.Kw. V'

Fletcher, David, 'British Panthers' in *Wheels and Tracks* No. 62, pp.16–25

'Conclusions to F.V.P.E. reports Nos FT.1391 & WS.413 on German (Pz.Kpfw) Panther Performance Trials and Workshops Report', DTD (12 June 1944, 14 June 1944 and 28 July 1944)

DTD Armour Branch Report M6815A/3 No. 1, 'Armour Quality and Vulnerability of Pz.Kw. V Panther', Department of Tank Design (1944)

'Fighting Vehicles Proving Establishment Automotive Wing Report On Panther – Performance Trials', FVPE Chertsey

'Fighting Vehicles Proving Establishment Field Trials Report on German Panther (Pz.Kw.V)', FVPE Report No. F.T.1391

Francis, E., 'Tortoise vs Panther: Design & Development', *Armoured Archives* (YouTube Channel) (24 September 2021)

'Mediterranean Area AFV Technical Report #27', Italy (1945)

'Military Operational Research Report No. 61 Study No. 11 issued by Motion Study Wing, Motion Studies of German Tanks'

The 503e RCC's Panthers were present at the Bastille Day parade on 14 July 1951. However, they were stationed in a static display around the Arc de Triomphe – there was no question of having a German machine parade through Paris so soon after the war. In contrast, the new AMX 13 and AMX 50 prototypes, as well as the 503e RCC's ARL 44s, paraded in neat formation down the Champs Elysées. Nonetheless, at the end of its service with the 503e RCC in 1952, there was a higher number of operational Panthers than of the new ARL 44s. (Fond Dubarry, Collection du Musée des Blindés de Saumur)

Samsonov, Peter, 'A German Cat in King George's Court', *Warspot* (https://warspot.net), 3 May 2021

'Tactical & Technical Trends' No. 37

'Tactical & Technical Trends' No. 40

'War Diary, The Seaforth Highlanders of Canada, October 1944', National Archives of Canada

US sources (NARA)

US Army 1944 Firing Test No. 1 (Shoeburyness, 23 May 1944)

'Report on Comparative Firing Program Witnessed at Shoeburyness, Essex, 23 May 1944 by U.S. Army Headquarters ETO representatives', Armored Fighting Vehicles and Weapons Section, APO 887.319.1 (24 May 1944), United States Army, England, 1944

(76mm M1, QF 17-pdr (Mk.I), 75mm (Mk.V) tested vs RHA plates to simulate anticipated German tank armour)

US Army 1944 Firing Test No. 2 (Balleroy, 12 July and 30 July 1944)

'Firing Tests conducted 12–30 July 1944 by 1st U.S. Army in Normandy: Report of Proceedings of Board of Officers', Headquarters, First U.S. Army, APO 230, United States Army, France (1944)

(Panthers tested vs Launcher, Rocket, AT, 2.36in. – Rocket, AT, 2.36in., M6A1, Launcher, Grenade, M8 – Grenade, AT, M9A1, 37mm Gun, M6, Mounted on Light Tank, M5A1 – APC M5, Bofors 40mm Gun, M1, AA – AP M58, 57mm Gun, M1 (ATG) – APC M86, and APDS, 75mm Gun, M3, mounted on Medium Tank, M4 – APC M61 and HEAT M66 (Special), 3in. Gun, M5, mounted on Motor Carriage, M10 – APC M62 with BDF M66A1, and AP M79 90mm Gun, M1A1, AA – AP M77, 105mm Howitzer, M4, mounted on Medium Tank, M4 – HEAT M67)

US Army 1944 Firing Test No. 3 (Isigny, 20 & 21 August 1944, reported 22 & 30 August 1944)

'U.S. Army Firing Tests conducted August 1944 by 12th U.S. Army Group at Isigny, France', Board of Officers, APO 655 (30 August 1944), United States Army, France (1944)

(Panthers tested vs 76mm M1, QF 17-pdr in Sherman Firefly)

Gallagher, Lieutenant-Colonel W. J., 'Effect of 90mm Gun on Enemy Tanks', Headquarters 628th Tank Destroyer Battalion (SP), United States Army (8 December 1944)

Moran, Nicholas, 'The Chieftain's Hatch: US Guns, German Armour, Pt 1 US Army Anti-Armor Firing Tests of 1944', https://worldoftanks.com/en/news/chieftain/chieftains-hatch-us-guns-vs-german-armour-part-1/

Stiver, Major E. N., 'Memorandum to 5th Tank Destroyer Group: Bazooka Test on Mk.V', United States Army (15 December 1944)

Wadle, Major L. J., 'Report of Effectiveness of 57mm Antitank Gun Against Enemy Armor', United States Army (12 December 1944)

Romanian sources

'Armata Romana 1941–45 by Horia Vl', Serbanescu, Cornel I Scafes and Co

CIA reports

CIA-RDP83-0415R005700190008-1, 'Shipment of Munitions to Hungary and Bulgaria; Shipment of Oil Products from Romania to Czechoslovakia' (21 July 1950)

CIA-RDP82-00046R000500410006-5, 'Romanian and Soviet Order of Battle', (15 November 1955)

Czechoslovak sources

Dubanek, Martin, *Od Bodaku po Tryskace: Nedokoncene ceskoslovenske Zbrjni Projekty 1945–1955*, Mladá fronta (2011), ISBN: 978-80-204-2515-7, pp.193–202

Francev, V., *Czechoslovak Tank Forces 1945–1992*, Grada, Czech Republic (2012)

Turza, P., *Tanks of German origin in the Czechoslovak armament. Army 1945–59*, Military History 2 (1998), pp.98–102 (drawn from the resources of MNO)

CIA reports

CIA RDP80-00810A000700070001-6, 'Czechoslovakia: Movement of Military Production to Slovakia (10 April 1953)

CIA RDP80-00810A003700130009-8, 'Czechoslovakia: 31st Heavy Artillery Brigade in Vyskov (8 February 1954)

CIA RDP82-00457R004200710004-7, 'Czechoslovakia: Tank Regiment 1 at Strasice (8 February 1950)

French sources (DGA)

Marest, M. and Tauzin, M., *L'Armement de Gros Calibre. Comité Pour l'Histoire des Armements Terrestres Tome 9*, Centre des Hautes Études de l'Armement, Division Histoire, France (2008)

'Le Panther 1947', Ministre de la Guerre, Section Technique de L'Armée, Groupement Auto-Char, France (1947)

'Note No. 29979 SEA/1, 19 Juin 1945' and 'Étude de Matériel 75 Raye des Chars PZ.KW5 et 3. Seances du 31 Juillet 1945', Établissements d'Expériences Techniques de Bourges, DEFA, France (1945)

'Notes d'interrogatoire de l'ingénieur en chef MAIER, responsable d'études chez ZF' (16 July 1945)

ETBS, 'Note sur l'étude du fonctionnement de la bouche à feu du Panther' (14 September 1945)

Ministère de la Guerre, 'Commission Permanente des Essais – Note de Renseignement sur le char Panther étudié par le 6e RC' (31 January 1946)

AMX, 'Note sur la Présentation en Recette des Chars Panther' (5 August 1949)

AMX, 'Note sur la Recette des Chars Panther sur le camp de Mourmelon' (3 October 1949)

AMX, 'Compte rendu de la présentation en recette des tubes d'artillerie du char Panther' (21 October 1949)

DEFA, 'Note sur le Contrôle des Recettes des Chars Panther' (5 December 1949)

AMX, 'Note sur la Présentation en Recette de Chars Panther' (8 December 1949)

AMX, 'Note sur le Contrôle des Bouches à Feu des Chars Panther' (29 December 1949)

AMX, 'Note sur la Présentation en Recette des Chars Panther (10 January 1950)

AMX, 'Note sur l'Embarquement VF des Panther Rénovés' (25 January 1950)

VIe RM/EM 3e bureau, 'Note sur les Essais de Panther sur le camp de Suippes (25 February 1950)

Technical manuals (translated from German into French):

DEFA, 'Char Panther – Schéma d'équipement électrique'

DEFA, 'Manuel de Conduite et d'Entretien du Char d'Assaut Pzkw. V Panther' (1 April, 1944)

DEFA, 'Notice Provisoire sur la Tourelle et l'Armement du Panther'

CIA reports

CIA RDP82-00457R005500200002-1, 'Syrian Arms Purchases' (10 August 1950)

INDEX

Page numbers in **bold** refer to illustrations, some caption locators are in brackets.